i built a boat with all the towels in your closet

(and will let you drown)

Previous To the Lighthouse
Poetry Publication Prize Winners

i built a boat with all the towels in your closet

(and will let you drown)

poems

Leia Penina Wilson

Red Hen Press | Pasadena, CA

Book design by Li Pallas
Layout and cover design by Michelle Olaya-Marquez
Cover image by Alex Hazlewood

Library of Congress Cataloging-in-Publication Data
Wilson, Leia Penina.
  I built a boat with all the towels in your closet (and will let you drown) : poems / Leia
Penina Wilson.—First edition.
    pages cm
  ISBN13: 978-1-59709-539-6 (paperback)
  I. Title.
  PS3623.I57 A6 2014
  811'.6—dc23
                        2014914781

The Los Angeles County Arts Commission, the National Endowment for the Arts, the Pasadena
Arts & Culture Commission and the City of Pasadena Cultural Affairs Division, the Los Angeles
Department of Cultural Affairs, and Sony Pictures Entertainment partially support Red Hen Press.

The publication of this book was made possible by A Room of Her Own Foundation's To the
Lighthouse Poetry Publication Prize, awarded in 2012 for the best unpublished poetry collection
by a woman.

First Edition
Published by Red Hen Press
www.redhen.org

acknowledgments

A special thanks to the persons and journals who first published some of these poems in one form or another:

Alice Blue Review, Burnt Bridge, The Chariton Review, Crab Creek Review, dancing girl press, *decomP magazinE, elimae, Handsome, Heavy Feather Review, Interim,* Mud Luscious Press, *Parcel.*

All my gratitude to Red Hen Press and to Evie Shockley for supporting this project. I would also like to thank A Room of Her Own Foundation and their Poetry Publication Prize for all the support and recognition they bring to the work of women writers.

To all the lovely people who encouraged me & tolerated my personality & ate cake with me:

Brandi Wells, for ignoring me that day in the airport, for sitting next to me later that same weekend, for having many a stout drink with me.

Aaron Barnett, my love, for all of it.

Michael and Ray, for keeping it real & for just being my brothers, thanks for teaching me Magic and giving me my first deck.

Mom, for your strictness, for never letting me quit anything, for teaching me the value of education, and working so many hours that I can have the opportunity to pursue it.

The Barnetts, for your warmth and welcome.

Professors Linda Seidel, James D'Agostino, Cole Woodcox, and Natalie Alexander, for your unfailing patience. To the entire English faculty at Truman State University, and thanks also to the McNair Program and Sarah Hass.

Thanks to the kindred spirits at the University of Alabama who read and commented on some of these poems. A special thanks to Matthew Mahaney, for your feedback during the making of this animal, thanks for always being frank.

for you

table of contents

i built a boat with all the towels in your closet

(and will let you drown)

lazy magnolia let me

i am looking for something to keep me warm in the winter / when the sky lets loose snow and all its other feelings

i have found a city. a solid hydrodynamic sphere / with mailboxes and daylight and stampedes of regular people who want to be in love.

purple / cerulean / sapphire. people who want to be in love only for a little while in order to experience *vectors*—and *mapping*—the transfer

unique bacteria from one human hand to another human hand: to practice thunder and length and echo— *echo*: the ability to capture a person

echo *touch*—a photographic memory: fluttering birds thirst to get away undigested and almost intact.

i have learned to synthesize it and

i am standing on my feet
    and my feet are pressing against the concrete

                how else am i to acquire *resistance*.
                all women

should learn how to stand *straight*   they can understand: *vicious*   *aftermath*

   and remain: upright appropriately naked legs parted
      or apart symmetrically faithful to subtle violence which is still violence
   but slower *slower*.

i wonder what this has turned me into:

        always on the look-out for dangerous sudden things and never
        remembering why it must be public.

        i used to dream that i was a troll.
        because i do not dream now now i know for sure that i am a troll.
        my feet prove it—strong lasting stuff.

i worry sometimes that i am *too much* of a troll. it is risky
                to breathe out loud
        so i softly *softly* exhale
     (and my body does not move so much)

in the past women kept it from the outside by storing it on the inside.

they continually brushed out the tangles

in front of some mirror and then they would break the mirrors

so there were no witnesses.

this backfired because they would have to walk over the glass

pretending / it wasn't glass and that *sharp* was a cough: only sexual.

and that blood was not *blood*

lest their husbands figure out ontology:

the body knowing

where the body is. i have learned
to synthesize it and place all its powers of pleasing at my feet.
that's what it's about: *placement*—

where to place things and still appear human

it's about standing on your feet and breathing and staying alive *simultaneously*.
longer than any body else can stand on their feet

proving *once again* that *slower* is a more useful terror.
it is tangible something i can hand to people and say "here.
this is how the world is. how is the world."

she eats his heart she has two hearts she doesn't know which one to use she begins to call the second heart "little baby" or "blitzkrieg"

the figure she hides

he came back / and i wanted him / to look carefully closely at me—

to protect and tangle the figure—

she hides behind the tree because she understands the error of both *true* and *lust*:

every fifty years the bamboo bursts into flowers:

the desire of a girl to be a horse—

what can be cooked on a stick can be carved—why he

never brought anything up against his body—

and now i know why up against his body.

she found the animal. she held him hostage. she held him tight. oh so very tight. she frays—evolves wrong: she sets all niceties aside and has her way with him. he kicks. her lip is bleeding. she smirks. her smirk is wild. a little unclean. her teeth glitter. her saliva glitters—*it's better this way* she thinks. nothing worth having should ever be easy. somebody said that / everybody says that so it's true or doesn't have to be true. *don't fuss* she says *just relax* don't make me make you cry. she was ready for it to hurt. the mindlessness of it all woke her / excited her. she trembled slightly and whispered lips cracked *let me kiss you.*

with windows adjacent to the highway

the poet says it is little more than a cage very airy very light chassis—eden
is *here* in our imagination and mine is called summerlea and there is an ugly
grey building with 1950s stucco: the high ceiling his arms modify the apart-
ment the thought approved is lost: there is silence and gripping and silent
gripping saying *i've now located my body and wondered also why i evacuated it.*
lingering and shiny—there's frustrated touching touching frustratedly: and
then—morning—city—

how a paper crane became an organic bird

it flew as far away from me
        as it could get because
        it wanted to breathe
        and become something *other than*—
to have flesh / moisture.
              —it wanted
                    to go beyond real madness
              to understand *without*.
it had written on its wings
        to remember you it's my own body i touch.

i felt sorry for it and tried to explain
        that paper cranes don't grow up
        and they most certainly don't fall in love.
              how could a paper crane have feelings.
         and saying that i hurt its feelings. it replied *i am seeking*
             the crucial region of the soul where response is pitted against intimately
        implicated anteriors. it attempted
to revise itself wanting to look like everybody else: pregnant
            with different necessities but always
          always the return.

this is where confusion sleeps because i taught it that deep

deep inside we are all the same. i detached it—

    the only way i knew to make it stay quiet:

            to rinse and rinse and *rinse*

            and hang

            and bleach internally

                to make it *stay*—

    the little paper crane became hungry

            licking its lips.

        it wandered around the middle of the street

started eating the same stuff everybody else was eating

without knowing what it was and soon

    it starts to eat itself because it tastes

    just like all the other stuff.

it begins to hurt less.

this is how i taught it.

she loses her mind but this time it will be different

i'm bored / why do dreams elude: *reading requires a lot from the body*—

where do i store my fear?

some age & mostly used / another train car another train / the impertinence of my everyday life some-

times amuses sometimes bruises / how difficult it is to be & not disposable!

help me i can't find

my brush or i'd brush my hair / i irritate—irritated: i irrationalizes

i shake my head / i'm a dog / horse / bear / i shake again i'm a cat

i refuse to look for my brush / belongs to me so where.

this catastrophe / i touch body / something torches

where have i put the future / who misplaces future—

klutz-y cunt why can't i remember tomorrow now what happens if i lose that.

i wedge my bellybutton open / i probe / i probe

it's gooey ooey (yuck) how do i throw up with my hand like this why can't i throw everything up.

there's a draft.

i pokepoke*pokes*—there's a bit of splashing / splotching—i wonder if i'll catch cold if i should turn on

the heat.

she wanted something she would die for

he came & i wanted him she repeats she invokes
none of it made sense to her she stumbles

da-dum-da-dum-da-da-de-dum-dada

i will show you——let me
she heard a language

i will show you the names of things——
something pulled her hair & she despairs at the new day

da-dum-da-dum-da-da-de-dum-dada

the anxiety: what touches me——
short of breath i breathe in his mouth

he silences / my sadness breaks time turns it into a disaster
i'm alone & lost in fear the guiding principle prophesizes

i growl——sharp——play dead and he leaves
i'm alone &

how will they ever become clean

he's still
he doesn't

say anything.
she's frustrated

he won't
say anything

why's he
so still

and quiet and.

she smells
something akin

to vomit
but meatier.

she remembers
how much

she watched
him sleep.

she'd always
wake up

earlier. she'd
watch him

for hours.
sometimes she'd

check his
pulse gently

press her
tongue against

his neck.
why'd they

never understand
the other?

the things she does to herself

scrub face off

scrub-bah-dub-dub-rub-rub——i rubs

it smarts

some face comes off in hands

oh geez: i rub more than i meant to

i stare at it

flinch a little

sniff it

touch it ever-so-lightly with the tip of my tongue

my face is peel-y

some of it is just hanging there

i peels off

sticker-sound almost a slurp

i peel pieces off quick——makes the same sound duct-tape makes when yanked flesh

oh flesh

i blushes

flush my face down the toilet

flush toilet twice

the toilet water is pink flush again

i wonder if anybody will find my face & what they'll do with it

i draw on a new face &

have some trouble getting my eyes even my mouth symmetrical my nose is lost

kissing is gonna be weird——and probably a little goopy

i worry this new face looks too similar to my old one

i gets a perm no extensions no curls so many curls no dread locks no——no: i just brush my hair pull it

into braids secure it with pins

why they never understood the other's city

—something.
caught.
say:
wildness—

                                     where.
                                     is it.
                                     in.
                                     the wilderness—

she killed.
her.
lover.
                                     the distinction.
                                     wondered if.
                                     she felt.
                                     any.
                                     different.
                                     or less.
                                     appropriate.

she never.
intended.
to repeat.
the likeness.
                                     in.
                                     the distance:
                                     coldness.
                                     in reply:
                                     static.

i would.

be.

brave.

in the light.

yet.

the morning.

pivots.

—what.

kind.

of animal—

keeps.

track.

of the tame.

aggressively.

longing.

they walked.

arm and arm.

and.

they knew.

where.

the form.

disguises.

the names.

of.

things.

your.

                                                            name.
                                                    reminds me.
                                                            of.

and what
of it.
and of.
what.
is.
she suffering——

your.
name is.
unkillable.
she.
surrendered.
and wept and.
regretted.   the sunrise.
                                                        to bleed.
                                                            every.
                                                        w(here).
                                                        knowing.

exactly.
why.
it hurts.
so.
much.

                                                            a.
                                                        plain.
                                                        sort.
                                                    of bird.
                                                    spoke—
                                                        it's.
                                                    crass.
                                            and everything.
                                                a flower.
                                                    should.
                                            be / without.
                                                genius.

average for being unusually monstrous—neither one
willing to feed the sadness their sadness

in the academy

i learned *asymptope* and nobody ever fixed me:
                                    became a moist vertical mode
                    intending to attend university
            publishing indecipherable probabilities
                                from the margins of my notebooks
                        on the theory that everything is private everything.

then private became confusing or i was confused by it
                                    and couldn't tell the differences in grammar.

            so i took a test but testing *assumes*

                                and i failed
                                because my body articulated
                                a different grammar

        no longer certain about how
                        to take air into
                        myself
                and turn it into *breathing*
                                i was expelled—

    they said i could come back when i could afford it
                                and had learned *silence*.

she counts to ten. she's good at this game: he is found—*he's hers.* she hugs him tightly—so very tightly. amazing she thinks how close *hug* and *hang* are. she wondered who designed those words they horrified her so close. oh. oh why is she being so nice. why is she being a girl so in love. why does it always come down to that. she wonders what makes her a girl made her this way she rages they rage apart: *why can't she just have her way with me.* he bites her lip too hard intentionally breaks her but she is already a little broke / breaking. she graffiti'd up his face—he hears her bellow. & he thinks what's the difference *isn't it easier this way.* he smirks wildly insecure but clever but unsure but knows he made a mistake: *i didn't destroy this world our world. i just made it so nothing could survive.*

the painter paints the house mustard yellow

the alarm clock casual / accidental / trying to keep the day away / still making noise— / still making noise / *if only i had a vase* / somewhere out there / the thought of being with you / doesn't upset me: just don't open your mouth too much / really sing / so the muscles in your throat / are moving— / a song bird sings the only tone it knows / addresses its noise to the scholar / knowing she didn't have any patience to sift / the quiet / furious / clutter & collapsed / odd bleeding—kneading / i was waiting / making an effort / to figure out where/the enemy is: they're always right next to you unexpectedly close *why are they always the enemy* / it's a crisis ugly & inevitably means change & passion is painful often & she's sudden & unsavory & / movement signals an updraft—*here* / *my left lung* / *is yours*— / he rolls over in bed—the sun / scraps against the grasses and memorizes / the yank: the simile / the whole dumb lifetime saying what

she takes her clothes off and wonders if there's shame

there is wetness in the body.

a picnic table and clouds lots of clouds: and an equal amount of *animal*.

how to lick your fear and make it less afraid licking it.

reaching across the keyboard in search of new and varied wildlife—

i waited until you were asleep and i stuck my hand into your chest desperately struggling to find myself.

dark and humid and sticky and i couldn't stay long.

all the raw pieces asymmetrical clotted but despite its deformity whispering: *please do something to me please.*

in fact it is muscle

i pretend to be a fish & aren't floppy enough. i'm not the correct type of floppy.
i'm un-correct and pretentious
& i emit.

i record my fear on a napkin *how do fish do this*. i stare at some fish in a tank and watch. i feel like a
peeper. i like the teal ones & observe how in control of their floppiness they are. how their
floppiness is in fact muscle.

i record my fear on another napkin *how flexible their spines & whatnots must be to withstand so much
pressure.*

deciding i never want to be a fish i record that on a napkin *all that pressure on top beneath next to you
suffocating you.*

because i have too many fears i record *one fish two fish red fish blue fish*—

how do they cut through tell me—
he cried and i watched that too. i record that on a napkin too *i am unable.*

i pretend to be something else pretend to be.

i'm in steeler country and all their fans are at the market in the fruit and vege-
tables—looking for something green to throw into the risotto for dinner: my
heart is awake standing in direct sunlight / distracted by the buddha's hand
near the grapefruit: how am i supposed to eat that. black radishes chinese
okra bright yellow carrots faded yellow carrots purple carrots too dragon
fruit. something tells me dragons didn't actually eat this fruit: we're wander-
ing around the modernism art space downtown: no dragons here either—but
pigeons—but there is water and sound and affect.

i am looking for something to keep me warm
when the sky lets loose all its other feelings

missing most / the letters: *dear*—dearest—*my* love—attempting to survive re-entry: i would like to despair

only i am too tired and scars build character. why else starlings

a literary fascination? once / i witnessed a bird / lonely / without doubt / stuck-through by what you might call grammar: a device not knowing

how to respond / my fingers trickling

trickling down. not understanding lips are *wet*. lush. tangled. more lush. more tangled.

if it is possible to be more wet / that.

tulips are pretty / but only if you plant them before the frost. only if you let them be flowers/crying
in the absence of an address: *i want to go home.* but

i dropped a handkerchief and didn't know how to replace any of its insides didn't know where the noun
had gotten its adjective.

if only the weather: clearer more delicate——frost has come early this year. odd to be so quick

about naturalizing a power relationship. inelegant considering most of the universe is composed of
hydrogen and helium. the syntax of language is notoriously obtuse *even here.*

objective evidence makes one thing that. *that.* and another thing this. *this.*

sub-distinctions. no more changing colors——now only snow. squirming. dandelion
leftovers / unattractively still able to breathe / almost a thrill——

how i wanted that adjective

(to actually taste me).

because of flight (fright)

I.

i left a message on his machine: *this is my midsection*: it's hollow (some bird) it's hollow (an unpacked room) it's hollow (it never was see) *see how my body is dumb unbuttoned*—

II.

she took the emptiness into her lungs and coughed—she took the emptiness into her lungs and it caught—she took the emptiness into her.

III.

i remember us touching each other—

IV.

it's cold i shiver the wet stones are sharp / scratchy the water is also sharp / scratchy—there are goose bumps on my arms my shoulders are stiff my feet inarticulate: i was real in that moment—beware of the real: it's vibrant and tortured—they say not to look back be afraid of the real: i'm left disembodied his head sings unbodied down the river

V.

let me kiss your mouth again.

we lost the city we woke up

& propositional phrases

she whispers to him *will you plead for survival please*. she says she needs him needs the solitude needs— he whispers to her don't you want this to work. i thought we were in love. *i thought you loved me* i love you. he looks earnest/ sad/hurt/hurt. his humanness bewilders her—she panics & tries her best to hurt him. he hurts. he hurts more—there's an erotic residue. it's all over the floor everywhere. maybe it had been there for years & she was just now noticing—the horror dismantles her she writhes. she empties her pockets she swears she'll never tell. she uses lysol / bleach / paper towels—*why doesn't it smell clean yet*. how will it ever become clean again.

the painting / the thing / reduced itself / the emergence / of the possum
from morning—her mate: we couldn't / put her in the ground for a week /
because we didn't want her / to suffocate: / she sat in a box for three days /
before we were able / to put dirt on top.

how to no longer commit improbable mistakes

"she records" "every" "improbable mistake" "she's unfeeling" "closes" "her" "eyes" "closes her eyes" "to the world she knew" "before" "*she wants*" "she records" "that as the first" "mistake" "she's possessed" "it's dark again" "she punishes herself" "for wanting" "*i thought you were mine—*" "her soul" "longs" "*longs*" "she's at a loss" "she tears her soul apart" "with her teeth" "sits still because" "she's got" "no soul" "now" "now she feels like an animal" "now she is" "an animal" "she dazzles at her humanness" "she hunches" "animals hunch" "she records a new list" "*he can reach the top cabinet*" "*and put the maple syrup away*" "he can" "*take the stairs two at a time*" "*sometimes three*" "*will there always be that distance*" "why is he so warm" "*why is he always so warm*" "she records the cold" "i'll make this sonnet to contain you" "*i'll contain you*"

because it's a matter strictly of taste

what can the well-behaved know
ha! she mocks them calls them out

she has learned
mathematics she can draw diagrams

she draws a diagram:
get down on all fours.

get down on all fours.
her language learns *hunger*

& hungers.
never really expecting escape

an effort / an effect—directed towards absence:
be very still and everything'll be okay.

through the peeping glass

she finds a fossil
it's lodged in the gravel / sand / fish guts
she dislodges it
discovers this fossil is double-sided

it's dirty and has raccoon shit on it but she cleans it up
ties a red bow on it with red ribbon
she's not sure where the red ribbon came from doesn't inquire
(she knows there's plot)

it's a little sticky
she's not sure what to do with the fossil now
it's about nothing
by nobody

she didn't understand her desire to keep it

mundane and precious she questions
her ability to distinguish worth
she lays on her back the couch is comfy

looks to the ceiling
holds the fossil over her head arms stretched out

won't you tell me where's my future? she wants to find it.

# of torque in some color

she looks to the sky
dozens of tiny voyeurs
she curses them

their apathy their insistence
on the immediate and
their reluctance to interfere

she thinks about stuff
jellyfish foxes tiny
foxes kittens

oh

kittens are tiny foxes
how wonderful

she thinks about all
the tiny things she enjoys
cupcakes whoopie pies

m&m's

she thinks about interference
she often can't hear herself
that's interference right.

she's concerned the noise
in her is interfering
her everyday life
she's concerned her
everyday life is interfered.

how close it is to fear.

she howls.

all they do is watch
she watches them back
calls them names says
i'm gonna eat you are you
gonna run?

a history of the erratic

"everyone has a secret" "hers" "inside hers" "it's eating her" "from the inside" "that savage assailant" "it chews on her" "lungs" "makes breathing difficult" "exercise no" "the equation" "she can't" "find the equation" "she tries to scare it out" "everything fears" "applied all the tactics of old" "she hits herself in the face" "throws her body" "into a lake" "hot rocks" "slams her hand" "into the refrigerator door" "she's in pain" "her hand is cold" "she eats" "a taco" "some fried" "rice" "a bowl" "of banana foster flavored ice cream" "she tries to vomit" "fails" "laughs at the irony" "she eats" "the same things again" "again" "again but" "this time tops them off" "with ranch dressing and a few glasses of cheap wine" "she vomits" "searches her vomit" "for some secret" "any secret" "something warm" "something real" "*really real*" "*authentic*" "damn" "fuck" "she's not sure" "how many days left before complete digestion" "she's digesting herself" "she falls" "onto the bed to ponder" "the statistical likelihood of that" "the authenticity escapes her" "now she shines" "now she's sullen and" "she doesn't know" "what to do with herself" "she's a little erratic" "she refuses to look at herself" "refuses the look of it"

i am too afraid too afraid

i am too afraid—of snow to make an angel—afraid it will eat me up /
whole—the abstract: a quick—vivid—description standing outside in stock-
ing feet. the door locked: cardboard cutouts: breasts stapled to them—real
women as background content. i am afraid—of conductivity: *accretion*—the
sticking together—of things to make some bigger things better: what is the
thing we are making bigger: snowflakes—snowflakes: untaught fragments
never intending symmetry—what never intends symmetry—lose the sym-
metry—refer acoustically to the constraint—*life*.

her prepossessing posture

she was a wife and mother over and over again
over and over again receptive

                    she's now a small museum
                    holding lots of small collectables
                    wondering about the cost of things

she's too wide
in the darkness and still widening

                    the darkness says *you're not*
                    going to fit through that hole

why whole—

the incision
of the precise the cost

                    the immediate: *here*

but i was already
mediated: *she* a system of value—

                    valuables:

here you are *again here*—*eat this*
it's a poem *tastes a pear*—

                    where—

her address is 636 negley in a city:

                                        her address is separate
                                        from the full measure of her body: now
                                        the attention to light is calling

from the office window / hair estranged

one does not love and return
unmade by absence.

conversation on the terrace

how intimate asphalt—
tattoo-like with feet.

so unfriendly
and severe and
won't.

gum laden perhaps
afraid of touching
and also to be touched—

and groan.

your wretchedness
represents—

alas! asphalt

you have only to let the moon through how beautiful the impediment of the standstill bodies—*standstill*: the release wounded and almost motionless—they're in love with each other and they can't reach each other but they're doomed: i go walking into the woods but the wolf is gone so better monsters are lurking and i am also doomed: i am not safe because i no longer know what is after me: there's an obedience to: an obliviousness to: bound up in the obedience to *reject her* too. for the first time there is doubt of the physical self bound up in the quantum mechanics of the situation: if only *if only* the night would be more humid if only you would be here in the night and then maybe my luck would change and be less terrible than being alone but the misery of the world is bound up in the competence of the word itself *if*.

description of some building

"they talked" "about never" "wanting" "to be" "in a long" "distance" "relation-
ship" "it's late autumn" "why is autumn always so late" "she muses out loud the
condition of the world the weather it's different here" "i'm cold" "she named"
"her" "desire" "*she*" "named hers" "what" "did you" "invite in" "she's baffled at
herself" "at her" "impasse—" "mexican standoff—" "momentarily" "romantic"
"shit:" "the human" "impulse" "to" "expose" "i fell" "outside" "dropping" "off"
"my rent" "check" "scrapping" "my knees" "there was" "blood" "never" "want-
ing to" "be" "the subject" "never" "wanting" "you—you" "cannot" "break it's"
"yours" "yours" "my heart" "is" "yours"

the body with self

"against" "body" "against body" "against" "body" "body" "what" "an odd" "inquiry
don't" "you know what" "creature" "you are" "bespeckled" "atomic tangerine"
"it's time" "figure out" "your own" "allegiance" "well i suppose i" "can't" "say
much" "else" "without a demonstration and" "i'm too" "far" "away for that"
"you should go" "out" "to the garden" "and sit" "with the daisies and" "watch
the sunset"

"i admired the painting" "it looked like a mountainside" "had forgotten itself"
"words are not" "the same as paint" "they say that don't" "they always say" "a
word really" "is a" "unit" "of meaning—what's" "it mean to mean" "to me" "my
inability" "to produce" "a town" "he knew" "only" "how to" "invent" "words: i"
"laid" "my" "nakedness" "out on" "the bed " "to better" "observe" "its character"
"and affection" "it's different" "when you splatter" "words" "it's different when
you splatter" "than when" "you" "splatter" "paint"

i too miss the tenderness of survival

and the only two stars left in the sky distantly starve

I.

and the only two stars left in the sky secretly starve. trying to make something hurt requires patience prerogative and momentary flashes of physical honesty. making it impossible to forget all the long nights when i climbed inside and was safe inside you and began to understand the work required in loving a city but why. why was i without you / surrounded. weren't we that thing so true it is in danger of ceasing to exist. what is that *thing ceasing*—

II.

fierce heat leftover from last week's civil disobedience: having nothing left inside i moved out. i put my face close to the blood on the lips of my fore-fathers and licked. that's when i learned *hesitate* and other things huddled outside desire. and i couldn't help but cry because i recognized *empty*. i continue to cry until the pain becomes tiny: then i swallow it and am able to say: *dangerous*. distance is *so dangerous* my love *you* are distant which is dangering. all the little pieces are inside and on danger: how do i flee the fire.

III.

seeing a clearing in the woods i tried to get away but the darkness was
equinoctial and i grew inside myself without leaving a note behind to tell
people where i went. there were more trees inside of me than in the woods.
mine were not burning so contagiously: also not so leafy or green. i walked
around—suddenly—a bird hankered by—a bird with a butterfly in its
mouth: the butterfly was sweating and panting—its body scream wilting. it
wasn't going to win but i willed it so anyways: *move violently and thrash about.*
kick. and just as quickly its heart stopped beating or it gave up and the wind
kept supporting the bird. a fragment of its wing fell to the ground.

IV.

i touched it carefully but i couldn't make it work: i couldn't make it work.

she adjusts herself: voice flesh

reading requires
a lot from the body: where
do i store my fear—

—hear—

how do i really moan
if knowledge
      is the bird beneath
         its feathers.

fissures opened in conflict

you will hate   birds because   they are

       beautiful

          and you can   never   be

                                    a bird.

       perhaps you can

          be   beautiful or——

uncertain galatea   why   do you induce   such violence——

you will hate that   too——

          the   mating   life

     is an erasure——bluish   and dispensable

                                  (what isn't
                                  dispensable?)

and a mysterious alteration   to plain-speak

please speak plainly.

historically   hysterical

there's an assertion   unaided by   i   —an eye—   and i

am also   self-conscious   about truth.

post it note

i cannot afford silence
it does not make money
or demonstrate the curiosity
of the well stated thing: the meanness
of the temporary side effect: *it is too close*
so i can't see it so i move away—still can't see it
an indication of something going on
that isn't captured
by the theory
but what isn't captured by the theory.

because of the distance it is difficult to grope

she felt naked their first winter / away from the city the stars—cleaner /
the wild grown over itself lost / the house it stood in front of her / door
unhinged but her enemy/his features distracted.

she thinks if only/if only i could get nearer. / she thinks where'd the
distance come from / there aren't any roads that lead here / how did he
get so far away. how can she possibly breach this expanse. she wonders if
she falls if it'll hurt enough if.

she undressed / she's naked/she hoped / you could hear her / she broke.

she summons all the power of romantic plot—

something chokes. she tries to think of something to say but.

she broke your favorite vase / it had your mother's ashes in it now / now
your mother is all over the floor / all over she laughs twirls in circles /
arms to the ceiling saying see house / *see how i will not buckle* / see now my
nakedness / she lays it out for him / how better to observe her character:
/ he says *i looked through the entrails of that animal to find you—look what i've
done to my hands. look what you've done.*

she lays herself out on their bed / she arches her back / flops back into the
pillows / the sheets / sighs / she repeats a historically accurate action / and
pulls at her hair / pulls all her hair out / now she is bleeding everywhere /
unattractively soaked / and unforgiveable.

the quiet boom is the most best boom

"she"

"finishes"

"wiping"

"the"

"blood"

"off"

"her"

"hands"

"and"

"hides"

"once"

"more"

"her"

"machete"

"in"

"the"

"piano."

an interrupt

what happens when her voice gets stuck in another voice's mouth and that
voice says tenderly "my dear you smell strongly of the outside:" in a whisper
because you are weak and your weakness appeals to my weakness and your weakness is
an appeal to my weakness and my weakness is appealing and my weakness is appeal-
ingly weak.

she started her body in public

she startled her body

she wasn't people were

to fill the sadness

her sadness the sadness

oh such a sadness

he startles the wilderness

out of it into it it's unclear unclothed

she shows him around the city

here she says *here's your city*—

here i will teach you to transfer heat

learn about heat.

the body knows *the body knows* she repeats: i want

a midwestern day without trees

he repeats *what midwestern day doesn't include trees?*

something grazes her insides:

why's it always like this

what's this permanence—why do i distrust it—

she sighs.

he sighs.

how to let it float near the surface visibly

surfacing visibly looking like need—

they never.

at some point they will ask you who you are

i dreamt mary carmichael:
a twentieth century post-modern body
and beauty
and woman: she synthesizes

if they capture you you talk—

pulled me through the lips of her vulva and
showed me my soul—*darkling who are you*
every morning—

she would always cry before her body:

when she was finished crying she would brush her teeth:
when she came out of the bathroom or closet
or sometimes she would sit in the hallway of the apartment

i would kiss her:

undress her softly
and focused: bite her bottom lip—
draw her attention away
from the certainty of her figure—

whatever that place was—i feared it—us:

so i bite her again and again
tell her i dream of her and closer
and closer——a small dismissal
of a missing girl crying out——

caught in the intensity of her own pleasure

the only way to affect density—

i seem to be continuously reaching

across the keyboard in search of new

and varied wildlife but i have lost surprise:

the first step of making a verb a noun.

i waited until you were asleep

and i stuck my hand into your chest

desperate

desperately struggling to find myself.

it was dark and humid and sticky

and i couldn't stay long.

all the raw

hugged tightly afraid

to fall out—but then i felt it:

moist as everything else in there

but rarer: more red: almost too hot

to be contained by anything living

except without it nothing else

inside you would work.

he spends the week with birth constant incessant birth that's how we know the mother because she's connected to an idea that believed in the earth and other improvisations: alabaster sort of beloved through time: critiquing the use of her the beauty moves uselessly opposed: she's an ideal that the poet carved into the perfect shape of himself and then he killed himself in response—*how do i bury her body in this weather.* her burden entirely dependent on—does he engage in that voice (soft as it is) coming from her mouth: indeed she knew how to feed herself / that's where he learned it: the distance was once charming but now now it charms and i am not sure if i should allow it: call it comic—obsessively lean—argue technique over consent—the trick: *kissing* is very environmentally dependent the romantic ideal a victim of both fables: white room with lights all lights completely out both rooms saying *we tested it on them because there was no law against it.*

the seam of her eyes admits / uneven solitude: stitched sunshine / into a letter into glass / stitched into his hand / a heaven—*uneven.* / up the ladder: up later: expressions / *allow* her face. / allow *her.* / of the light. the seam. the uneven. / the glass a bird began crossing.

he was not whole— / such a little dinosaur—how fast / how invisibly he was frightened / but still *bird* still—he dreamt: / he went up—flew just / an iris: / the will to. / the will of her eyes in his hand: *un-stitched.*

a brief definition—the cause / of danger: the bird wanted / the un-stitching himself: he dreamed about that too. of the privilege / of the choices—of it all

he had seen her singing and become / very sad but if her words or / his mood it's unclear: everything *everything* was so sweet / and light / and stunned by hunger: / the will to: / stunned by *being:* / the will of—

his chirp awkward and un-amusing

her tone leaky and absurd: / the absurdity of it in minding / the gather-round so as to say—it's easy / if everything goes according to plan: / apply only a slight amount / of force to visible dreams: / it changes only the texture.

portrait of a lady reassembled

her lover task-oriented / the result of practicing sex and their fear.

intimate gender—— / brightly polished / ever new——

a non-discreet woman clothed / in non-discreet clothes.

the risk: any moment / the fictional significance of trains——

she also has hips—— / a mysterious cutlery: suggesting splendor and an imperious and / self-possessed cheek / she's got lots / of cheek

she also has a mouth / called *instrument*——lips ajar / it often says: *in order to understand world* / *knowledge*

a thing a verse——against her / colors are evoked by light are——

surgically / others by sound: the spit of the body——

something spits: oh tense afternoon! / limited sunshine limiting space——and texture

all rooms occupied——sadly / without remorse or composure: of torture——

the ambiguous contour of most anywhere

not alone   or
lonely   or any
of the orderly   things
that make
other   things
mean   ing   ful
in the lives   of living   people.

    leaving   you
    it
    just   leaves
    you.

      surrounded
        by   leaves
      just falling: where
        am   i
      supposed to   go
        when i'm   surrounded.

where
is
my
loyalty
in   leaves.

where

        is

    my

  loyalty

      to

 your
 body

in
leaves.

w(here) is my loyalty to.

the elsewhere or with one foot on the ground she listened
to his sensitivity his smell

i am looking for something to keep me

oh! how i would graft my face into your forest. maybe i can

be a moon or a star or a constellation. something made of light. something made of heat—touchable—so
that *consume*—and then i could write

the line *what strength when we cast each other*

there's the shadow / for no other reason than to have your hands (re)arranging me. oh dearest how i would
like my lips to meet yours and your lips to meet mine and the pair of us would fall

an aftermath / without complete sentences / almost senseless / almost.

and the world would be quiet / fearing to interrupt.

and we lost the city we woke up in

i built a boat with all the towels in your closet &

it will be a soft trip to somewhere or

i kept your key around my neck so that one day i might return it

                                    and removed all the doors from the house &

i stayed up for two days hoping to be obvious and a little pathetic

——*or*——

i threw all your shoes in one pile in the right corner of the dining room and left a note: *this is a form /
my form.*

& the panic i feel to return home in the dark *can't you hear the sound—it's such a sound—*spontaneous
degradation: the cicadas outside shed their skin and are shiny.

& i crawled inside you and took off all my clothes and still couldn't exorcise your heart.

& i stretched and remembered why we never groped each other fondly—

there was no letter today: my love *what* is this love i shall never tease about it again—

& failing the exchange of absence—intimate flight *how could you.*

&.

and you returned

and wondered why i thought it belonged to you *why i thought it belonged to you*—lazy magnolia let me no longer imprison you: & lying in bed the roughness of the terrain seems unintentionally imposed—exposed / are they really they diffident.

& the weather hasn't been good for hiking since july and here it is august. & i forgot my boots they're in your hallway though i think it might be awkward / now / to come over and retrieve them.

"i sobbed" "under" "the moonlight" "the night" "when" "the meteor" "shower" "was supposed" "to be brightest" "under a" "tree" "next to" "that place" "we" "drank coffee" "every evening" "after" "work" "some people" "cower" "she waited" "sound" "hurtled by" "her" "hid" "her" "she never" "wanted" "that" "to be" "that person" "loud" "it's expensive" "to" "admit" "they knew" "where" "the other" "was" "vulnerable"

conversation on terrace: a block away

a pleasure lingering
on specific moments of contact—

asphalt: a lingering pleasure

very specific: more
rudely than / more eloquently than:

—it is too difficult to translate:
children are
bloody and
alive and undone—

urgently new—

last night's assault—
rather lonely—oh the splendor!

how to hold
onto things when the drag—
a whole bunch of big words
using the same line: fair
rosy white cheeks: *fair rosy white cheeks*

all wanting repetition—
repetition—how do you execute a dash.

because weight is distributed differently when afloat

she contracted—extracted—

she put her loneliness in an airtight jar and set the jar afloat.

he found her loneliness (its airtight jar). fished it out of the sea (unknowingly hungry for it).

unsure about *ravage* or *rage* but he opened her.

he built a city upon a hill with her loneliness (out of it). destroyed all the roads and railways to the city—
it was his city (a secret city).

what do you do with a city that's all a secret she wonders do we even exist?

eventually there is some light

she stares at her new face in the mirror for half an hour / she eventually turns on lights / looks again into mirror / scowls at light / *look what it's done to her* / her left eye smeared / she redraws it and thinks emptiness's / remembers reading something about women of antiquity having to paint their bodies / *they'd know if somebody touched the one that was theirs they'd be smeared* / she must look as if she belonged to everybody at once / she was so blurry / she didn't think she'd ever get used to applying her face every day (maybe three or four times per day) but now she didn't have much choice / she's almost sure the world looks a little different but if pressed she couldn't tell you how exactly / she wonders if she'll pass herself on the street someday / if she'll recognize herself / she is unrecognizable at the moment / you wouldn't recognize her

i tried to show her how to seduce the outside but

because it is a rose she said: other flowers have twelve decimal places/but
a rose: a rose only has four—easier to re-member and sometimes inventive
when *dangerous* is a necessary verb: when is dangerous a necessary verb—

and still she dreams dreams

how it strangles & pulls she's open / is there fear. can there be fear. she's unable to feel she's overwhelmed / she's unconscious / daily life is too much when did she become so weak she doesn't

she dreams a dream of him: he is open why is there no sound no silence shouldn't he be making some sound some tiny silence—*he is open* / organs pronounced pulled *did she do this?* her memory is unfocused

she kneels beside him tries to shove it all back in she didn't mean it she didn't mean she didn't mean to make things so visceral she didn't mean it

she flails she fits

she repeats *i didn't mean it what didn't i mean i mean didn't i*—she tries to make him whole again / she dirties her hands how did all this stuff fit in there in the first place *he's so tiny* / how could there be so much liquid in one body his hair was soaked with it it clings to her fingers between them she's unsure how much of it she's actually putting back in

she suddenly remembers baking bread and curses herself / she suddenly remembers they exchanged words he took hers hostage she remembers the sentence *i feel so untouched*—who owned it?

everything was distrustful to him to her the selfishness of her feelings cradles her startles her she forgets she forgot *i'm lonely*

she suddenly remembers she's supposed to scream why is she so calm

"the hummingbird" "outside" "my window" "gnawed at" "some inedible" "look-
ing berries" "majorelle blue" "the color of" "fake frost" "there was frost" "our
first" "winter away" "from the city" "the stars" "are cleaner" "i remember your"
"first poem" "to me the tiny" "paper crane you" "left on your pillow" "when
you went" "a walk" "in the middle" "the night and" "had wrote on its wing"
"*touch*—" "which in the middle" "of the night" "i" "read as *tooth*"

and become exhausted by the visible

there's not much you can do
        as it turns out
        everything else a variation
            alighting under trees
            hoping for the best as you get down on all fours.

now coincidence: i get down on all fours
        and think about animals
        the ways they are born
        the ways they are nurtured
                to know about pleasure. there are no choices
in nature only: *to be taken over.*

how to get out of heavy winds:
        the hollow of my thigh could nest them
        they might also eat it
        being of the wild and seeing
        an opportunity to survive.
            then they would no longer be *wedged*—

the animals could then be *beasts*
        but there's only one freefall—she
            has the power of authority
                because
        it is denied her
        and she reflects on it:

the animals

they'd go into the actual world: ripe——and: more eating

and become

exhausted by

the visible.

and it would still be about power would it.

and you would still breathe

differently down there

and he would have still slept with the name of her.

biographical note

Leia Penina Wilson recently graduated with her MFA from the University of
Alabama. She's since then moved to the desert, and will be pursuing her PhD
in poetry at the University of Las Vegas, Nevada. She's proudly Samoan, and
is thrilled to find taro in the grocery stores. When she's not writing she likes
to play Magic the Gathering, watch movies, make cocktails, and bake.

Printed in the USA
CPSIA information can be obtained
at www.ICGtesting.com
JSHW060042150824
68134JS00028B/2602